THOMAS CRANE PUBLIC LIBRARY

QUINCY MASS

CITY APPROPRIATION

Learning About the

Human Body Systems

Learning About the Musculoskeletal System and the Skin

by Susan Dudley Gold

Enslow Publishers, Inc.
40 Industrial Road
Box 398
Berkeley Heights, NJ 07922
USA

http://www.enslow.com

Dedicated to my parents,
Edward and Helyn Dudley

Acknowledgments

With thanks to: My husband, John, for his help and support in writing this book. Carl Spirito, Ph.D., associate professor of physiology, College of Health Professions, University of New England, for providing resources and advice for this book.

Library of Congress Cataloging-in-Publication Data:

Gold, Susan Dudley.
  Learning about the musculoskeletal system and the skin / Susan Dudley Gold.
    p. cm. — (Learning about the human body systems)
  Includes bibliographical references and index.
  Summary: "Find out how this marvelous system works and learn some interesting facts about muscles, bones and skin" — Provided by publisher.
  ISBN 978-0-7660-4159-2
  1. Musculoskeletal system-—Juvenile literature. 2. Skin—Juvenile literature. I. Title.
  QP301.G57 2013
  612.7—dc23

                2012011102

Future Editions:
Paperback ISBN 978-1-4644-0239-5
ePUB ISBN 978-1-4645-1156-1
PDF ISBN 978-1-4646-1156-8

Printed in the United States of America

082012 Lake Book Manufacturing, Inc., Melrose Park, IL

10 9 8 7 6 5 4 3 2 1

To Our Readers: We have done our best to make sure all Internet addresses in this book were active and appropriate when we went to press. However, the author and the publisher have no control over and assume no liability for the material available on those Internet sites or on other Web sites they may link to. Any comments or suggestions can be sent by e-mail to comments@enslow.com or to the address on the back cover.

♻ Enslow Publishers, Inc., is committed to printing our books on recycled paper. The paper in every book contains 10% to 30% post-consumer waste (PCW). The cover board on the outside of each book contains 100% PCW. Our goal is to do our part to help young people and the environment too!

Illustration Credits: © Art Explosion, Nova Development Corp., pp. 21, 23; © Digital Stock, Corbis Corp., pp. 33, 34, 38; © Life Art, Williams and Wilkins, pp. 4, 7, 9, 10, 13, 14, 17, 20, 39; National Cancer Institute, p. 28; Shutterstock.com, pp. 1, 31, 40.

Cover Illustration: Shutterstock.com

Contents

SKELETAL SYSTEM, front view

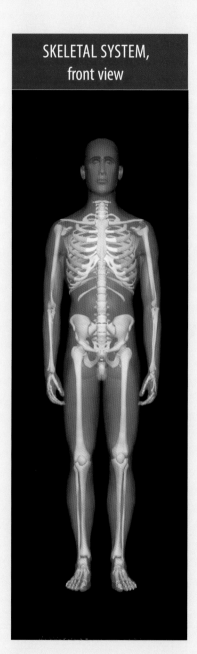

MUSCULAR SYSTEM, front view

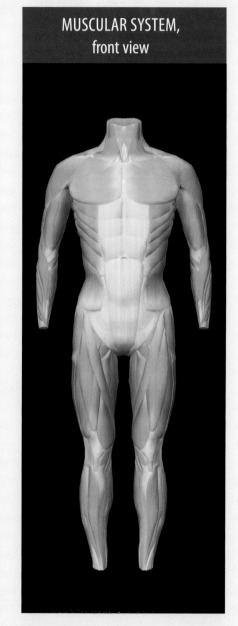

What Is the Musculoskeletal System?

Picture a house being built. Long, sturdy beams form the framework upon which the weight of the house will rest. Smaller beams and boards join the beams together and support windows, doors, and walls. Hinges allow doors to swing open and shut. Once the structure is in place, workers cover the framework with sheet rock and shingles.

Skeleton

The human skeletal system is much like the framework of a house. Like beams, the long bones of the legs, arms, and pelvis form the support structure of the human body. The bones also protect the body's vital organs from harm.

The skeleton is made up of two parts: the **axial skeleton** and the **appendicular skeleton**. The axial skeleton has eighty bones which make up the skull, the spine, and the ribcage. The 126 bones of the appendicular skeleton form the shoulders, pelvis, arms, and legs.

Bones consist of three sections. The outer layer, called the **periosteum**, covers the bone. This thin white layer of skin contains nerves and blood vessels that bring oxygen and nutrients to the bone. Beneath the periosteum lies the **compact bone**, a layer of hard, rigid material made mostly of calcium and minerals. Within the compact bone, nerves and blood vessels snake their way through a maze of holes and passageways. **Marrow**, a fatty substance found in the hollow center of the bones, produces red and white blood cells. Red blood cells carry oxygen to the rest of the body, while white blood cells fight infection. Much of the body's red blood cells are made in the marrow of the ribs. Spongy bone—thin bony material with hollows that resemble those in a sponge—surround the marrow.

The structure of bone allows it to support the weight of the body. Bone is made up of **osteocytes**, tiny bone cells. **Collagen** fibers fill the space surrounding these bone cells. These strands of collagen, a protein, make the bone flexible. Mineral salts of calcium and potassium, also in the bone, make the bone hard. This combination—strength and flexibility—allows bones to support up to four times more weight than concrete. In fact, bones are living cells, sometimes called "living concrete" because of their strength.[1]

BONE

consists of three layers:

1. periosteum, the outer covering

2. compact bone, hard and rigid

3. marrow, a fatty substance that produces red and white blood cells

Spongy bone placed strategically at the ends of the long bones absorbs much of the pressure from the body's weight and movements. Bone itself weighs little. Only about 14 percent of a person's body weight is from the skeletal system. That is because many bones are hollow. But one cubic inch of bone is strong enough to support ten small cars (from eighteen thousand to twenty-four thousand pounds).

Each bone's shape matches the job it has to do. For example, the femur—the thigh bone located between the pelvis and the knee—has a wide end filled with spongy bone to absorb pressure from the upper body. The long, hollow portion of the bone is rock-hard, strong enough to support the person's weight.

Muscles

Skeletal muscles allow the bones to move. By tightening and relaxing, these muscles let people walk, smile, play ball, eat, breathe, and do a thousand tasks that require movement. Almost 40 percent of a typical man's weight is from skeletal muscle.[2] An average woman's skeletal muscles account for slightly less of her overall weight.

The body has a muscle for every movement it makes. A person has about six hundred skeletal muscles, and each muscle has its own special job to do. For example, plantar **flexor muscles** turn the foot and the toes toward the floor. Something as seemingly simple as rolling one's eyes requires six muscles.[3]

Skeletal muscles are voluntary muscles, responding to a person's commands. For example, a ballerina who wants to stand on her toes signals the foot and toe muscles to contract and allow her to move her body upward. Skeletal muscles are made up of bundles of fibers. The largest of these muscles, like those in the buttock, contain hundreds of bundles. Tiny muscles, such as those in the ear or the eye, have only a few. Under a microscope, a skeletal muscle has a series of light and dark bands running across it, resembling the skin of a king snake.

Though most skeletal muscles move bones, some have other tasks. Facial muscles control expressions. Muscles open and close the eyelid, stop urination, and help eliminate wastes from the body, among other duties. Thorax muscles expand and contract as a person breathes. Sheets of muscles in the abdomen protect the stomach, the liver, the kidneys, and other organs.

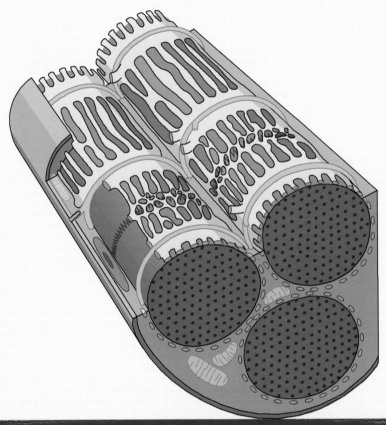

Skeletal muscle is made up of bundles of fibers.

In addition to skeletal muscles, a person has two other types of muscle: **smooth muscle** and cardiac muscle. Unlike skeletal muscles, smooth muscles contract and expand without a person's command. These involuntary muscles act even while a person sleeps. They control, among other things, the urge to urinate, the flow of blood through blood vessels, and the body's response to stress. Cardiac muscle, found in the heart, also acts involuntarily and controls the beating of the heart.

Skin

Skin plays the same role in the human body as sheet rock and shingles do on a building. Skin, the body's largest organ, covers the entire surface of the body. Like shingles on a house, it keeps water out and warmth in. And like shingles, it has to be replaced periodically.

Everyone has two layers of skin. The outer layer of skin, called the **epidermis**, is about .1 millimeter thick (about one-tenth the thickness of a dime).[4] It is made up of many cells, packed tightly together. These cells form one sheet of skin covering the body. This sheet of cells is watertight, airtight, and tough enough to protect the body from most chemicals

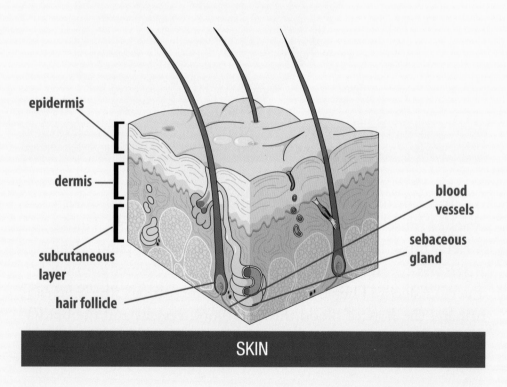

epidermis

dermis

subcutaneous
layer

hair follicle

blood
vessels

sebaceous
gland

SKIN

and other harmful substances. It also stands as a guard against disease. The skeletal system depends on the skin to provide vitamin D, which the skin produces by using energy absorbed from the ultraviolet rays of the sun. Vitamin D helps the body absorb calcium, which makes the bones hard.

The innermost layer of skin, called the **dermis**, is made up of fatty tissue, blood vessels, nerve fibers, and smooth muscle cells. Its job is to provide a person with a sense of touch. It also regulates the body's temperature, making sure a person doesn't become too hot or too cold.

The dermis also contains several **glands**. A gland is a cell or group of cells that makes certain substances and then releases them. There are two kinds of glands, endocrine and exocrine. An exocrine gland releases substances into ducts, while endocrine glands do not use ducts. All the glands in the dermis are exocrine glands.

The skin's glands are divided into two types: sebaceous glands and sweat glands. Sebaceous glands discharge oily fluid to keep the hair shiny and the skin soft. Sweat glands wet the skin with salty fluid to cool the body.

A loose layer of tissue and fat cells connects the skin to bone or muscle. This is called the **subcutaneous layer**, and it lies beneath the dermis. Most of the body's fat is found here.

Together, the skin, muscles, and bones make up more than 65 percent of a person's body mass. The structure of the bones, the flexibility of the skin and how it fits over the bones, and the shape of the muscles—all determine a person's looks, body type, height, weight, strength, and other physical features.

Who Is on the Team?

Chapter 2

The musculoskeletal system has many sections that work together to provide support and flexibility. Skin, bones, muscle, and related body parts are connective tissues that hold the body together.

The adult human skeleton contains 206 bones. At birth, a human has about 350 bones. Most of these bones are soft and flexible. As the baby grows, the bones harden, and many fuse together. In children, plates of **cartilage** are located at the ends of the long bones. This allows the bones to grow. Once a person becomes an adult, the bones stop growing and harden.

Bones do much more than support the body. Composed of living cells, bones make most of the body's blood cells and store a number of needed minerals. The long bones of the arms and legs, lightweight but powerful, act as levers. Flat bones cover the kidneys, the brain, and other organs and protect them from harm. Short bones give the skeletal structure its strength.

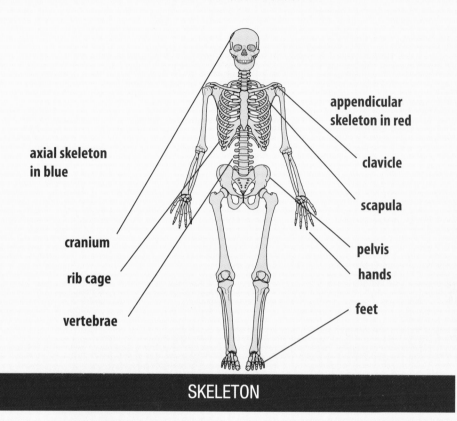

**axial skeleton
in blue**

**appendicular
skeleton in red**

clavicle

scapula

cranium

pelvis

rib cage

hands

vertebrae

feet

SKELETON

Axial Skeleton

The bones that make up the axial skeleton assume the role of
protector. The skull, including the eight bones of the cranium,
guards the brain. Flexible membranes connect the cranium bones
in the developing baby. This allows the head to squeeze through
the birth canal. These bones fuse together by the time a child
reaches age two and form the hard, immobile surface of the skull.

Serving as a coat of armor, the backbone surrounds the
spinal cord and shields it from outside forces. Thirty-three
hollow rings of bone, called **vertebrae** make up the backbone

and form a vertical column running from the skull to the pelvis. Like the main beams in a house, this bony, flexible column serves as the skeletal system's center of support.

The vertebrae are divided into five segments, each with particular tasks. At the top of the column, seven cervical vertebrae support the skull. These bones move when a person nods or swivels the head. Twelve thoracic vertebrae support the ribs and let the body bend forward and to the side. Set along the lower back, five lumbar vertebrae move the torso backward and sideways. At the end of the spine, five sacral vertebrae and four coccygeal vertebrae transfer the body's weight to the pelvis and the legs. In adults, these last vertebrae become fused to form one sacrum and one coccyx.

> **BACKBONE or SPINAL COLUMN**
>
> Thirty-three bony rings surround and protect the spinal cord.

Protecting the lungs and heart, the ribs form a cage around the chest organs. Men and women both have twenty-four ribs. All run from the spinal column and all but the lower two pairs of ribs (the "floating ribs") connect to a bony plate called the sternum (also known as the breastbone) in the front of the chest.

Appendicular Skeleton

The bones of the arms, legs, pelvis, shoulders, hands, and feet that make up the appendicular skeleton allow the body to move easily.

The arms are attached to the axial skeleton by two scapulas (shoulder blades) and two clavicles (collar bones), a pair on each side. The shoulder blade moves freely over the rib cage. This lets a person swing both arms in a wide circle.

The pelvic girdle (pelvis) sits on top of the leg bones. Together, the pelvis and the legs support the spinal column and the weight of the upper body. When a person sits down, the weight shifts to the chair or sofa where he or she is sitting.

Perhaps the two most remarkable systems of bones in the body can be found in the hands and feet. Together, the hands and feet contain more than half of all the bones in a person's skeletal system. Each hand has eight carpal bones in the wrist, five metacarpal bones in the palm, and fourteen phalanges in the fingers. Twenty-six bones make up each foot.

The hand, with its opposable thumb, can pick up something as tiny as a grain of sand and mold a lump of clay into a stunning piece of sculpture. Strong as well as precise, the hand can swing a hammer, pull a person to safety, and crush a can. More than thirty pairs of muscles control the hand's movements.

The foot, too, is a remarkable creation. A skilled architect could not have designed the bony structure of the foot any better. Like a bridge, the foot's twenty-six bones form an arch to support the entire weight of the body.

Joints

Bones join at a point referred to as a joint. Without joints, our bodies would be rigid, and we would not be able to bend, sit, walk, or chew. Like hinges on a door, joints allow the bones to move.

Cartilage protects and separates the two bones at the joint. This tough, smooth, elastic material covers the ends of most bones and keeps them from rubbing against each other. Each vertebra in the backbone is protected by a small disk of cartilage. Cartilage also makes up the tough outer ear and the end of the nose.

The joint is held in place by **ligaments**, which run along the outside of the joint. These short bands of tough, flexible tissue connect bones to other bones. Muscle is attached to the bones in the joint by tough strands of tissue called **tendons**. When the muscle contracts and shortens, the bones move.

Joints need lubrication to work smoothly just as rusty hinges do. The **synovial sac**, thin tissue lining the joint, contains a fluid

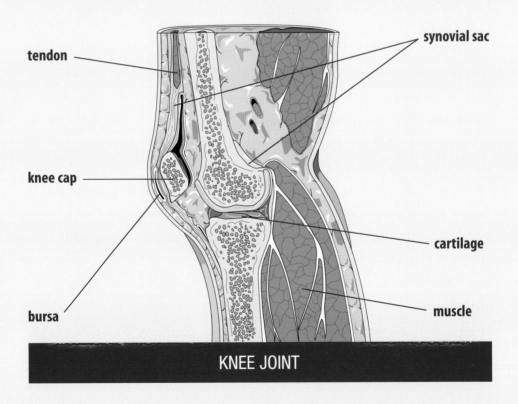

tendon

synovial sac

knee cap

cartilage

bursa

muscle

KNEE JOINT

that acts like oil to keep the joint moving freely. Joints that get a lot of use—knees and shoulders in particular—also have a **bursa**. This small sac of fluid near the joint provides more fluid to keep the joint "well-oiled." Without the fluid, friction would wear away the cartilage and the bones would eventually grind to dust.

Joints that allow the least movement are the strongest. The most flexible joints are also the least stable.[1] Among the strongest joints are those that join the plates of the skull. After a person reaches age two, the joints in the skull no longer move. The joints in the shoulder are among the most flexible. They allow a person to rotate his or her arm in a full circle. But the shoulder joint can also slip out of place. Shoulders and hips, which both rotate, use **ball-and-socket joints**. Other joints that allow back-and-forth movement are called **hinge joints**. Found in the knees and the elbows, they work much like door hinges that swing open and shut.

Epidermis and Dermis

The skin has its own set of key players: the epidermis, the dermis, and the substances linked to them. The cells in the lower layers of the epidermis constantly divide into new cells. These new cells push the older cells up toward the skin's surface. As they travel upward, the cells flatten and fill with a tough, disease-fighting protein called **keratin**. When they reach the outer layer, the cells—now dead pieces of keratin—form a protective cover to keep out water, air, and germs.

The fingernails and toenails are hardened keratin. Hair, too, is made of keratin. Each hair forms inside a **follicle**, a hollow chamber of epidermal cells. Cells at the base of the follicle divide into new cells. As the new cells pile up, they force older cells upward. These cells fill with keratin and harden. The hardened keratin becomes the shaft of hair that extends out of the skin.

A person's skin color depends on the amount of **melanin**, grains of pigment, in the dead cells of the epidermis. Skin with few of the dark granules will look pink when blood rushes near the skin's surface. This is what happens when someone is embarrassed and blushes.

The under side of the epidermis forms peaks and valleys that fit into the wavy surface of the dermis like matching puzzle pieces. The ridges in the layers of skin can be seen clearly in a person's fingerprints.

Beneath the surface, the dermis performs the skin's major work. As in bone, strands of collagen within the dermis strengthen the skin and hold it together. These fibers make the skin elastic. Despite parents' warnings that a silly face will freeze that way, collagen fibers ensure that the skin snaps back to its original shape.

The fatty tissue of the dermis cushions the body and keeps it warm. Blood vessels, nerve fibers, and smooth muscle cells all function inside the dermis. The blood vessels bring nutrients and oxygen to the outer skin. They also keep the body warm in cold weather and cool in hot weather. Nerve fibers give the skin its sense of touch. When a person touches a hot stove or stubs a toe, these sensors send the right message to the brain. The smooth muscles beneath the skin's surface control the flow of blood through the blood vessels. They also form goose bumps and make the hairs stand up on the skin when a person is cold or afraid.

How Does the System Work?

Chapter 3

Moving may seem like a simple matter. But in order to bend just one little finger, the body must call on a complex network of systems. The parts involved and the ways in which they act together are much more complicated than the motor that powers a car.

Marvelous Muscles

The chain of command begins with the brain. Let's imagine that a boy sees a fly ball heading his way and decides he will run and catch it. The brain issues the order: run. Nerve cells, or **neurons**, in the brain send out the message in the form of electrical impulses. In a flash, these electrical impulses travel down the spinal cord from one nerve ending to the next and into the muscles of the legs.

The brain sends out another order: catch the ball. Again, electrical impulses speed through the spinal cord. This time the message goes to the arm's muscles. The nerve impulses tell certain muscles to contract. The nerve cells that carry these

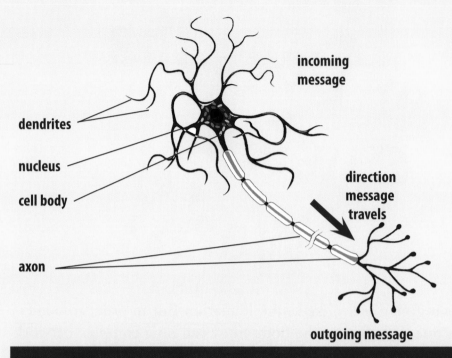

dendrites

nucleus

cell body

axon

incoming
message

direction
message
travels

outgoing message

MOTOR NEURON

messages to the muscles are called **motor neurons**. At one
end of the neuron, tiny branches called **dendrites** receive
the nerve impulse from other neurons. At the other end,
an **axon**—a thicker stemlike cord—carries the impulse to
muscle fibers. In response, the muscle fiber contracts. Some
neurons trigger only a few muscle fibers, like those that move
the eye. Other neurons trigger a response in hundreds or
thousands of fibers, like those in the calf where up to two
thousand fibers contract.

Skeletal muscles work in teams of two or more. Several
pairs of muscles go to work as the boy begins to run and as
he lifts his hands up for the ball. When he bends his arm to

position it under the ball, the biceps muscle on top of the upper arm shortens. This type of muscle, that bends an arm or leg at the joint, is called a flexor muscle. When the biceps muscle shortens, it forces the arm to bend at the elbow, pulling the lower arm upward toward the shoulder.

At the same time, the triceps muscle under the upper arm relaxes. When the arm is straightened, the bulging biceps muscle relaxes and the triceps shortens. The triceps is an **extensor muscle**, which contracts to straighten an arm or leg. Flexor and extensor muscles work together to move the bones of the body. Other sets of muscles in the shoulder lift the arm over the boy's head, while muscles in the fingers prepare to grasp the ball.

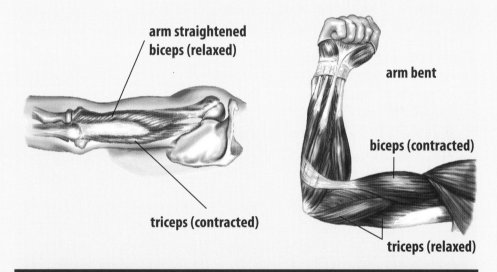

arm straightened
biceps (relaxed)

arm bent

biceps (contracted)

triceps (contracted)

triceps (relaxed)

ARM MUSCLES

The triceps, an extensor muscle, contracts to straighten the arm. The biceps, a flexor muscle, bends the arm when it contracts.

Still other muscles in the neck allow the boy to turn his head. Muscles in the head and eyes help him follow the ball's path and focus on it.

As he runs toward the ball, the boy uses several other sets of muscles. The long, powerful thigh muscles—some contracting, some relaxing—move the bones of the leg forward, while flexor muscles bend the leg at the knee and extensor muscles straighten it.

When a person picks up an object, muscles contract and shorten or lengthen to move the hand toward the object, to grasp it, and to move it upward. This type of muscle action is called **isotonic contraction**. But once the object is in the person's hands, the muscles no longer need to move anything. At this point, the muscles do not lengthen or shorten. But they tense to hold the object in place. This is called an **isometric contraction**.

Spectacular Skin

Back at the ball field, the boy reaches up and catches the ball in his glove. But wait! The ball bounces out of the glove. Quickly he grabs it with his other hand. The bare skin stings as the ball hits hard. The skin contains many cells called **sensory receptors**. Like reporters waiting for a story to break, the sensory receptors are on the alert for action. Once an action takes place, the sensory receptor assigned to that event sends its report to a nearby neuron, which transmits the "story" to the spinal cord and to the brain. Each sensory receptor is responsible for its own special type of action. Some respond to motion, touch, and pressure. Others respond to cold or heat. Still others react to pain, to light, or to certain chemicals. The sensory receptors in the boy's hand send out the message to the brain: ouch! Despite the pain, the boy holds onto the ball, and the batter is out.

Using Leverage

A worker uses a wheelbarrow to carry dirt, concrete, and other heavy loads from one place to another. The design of the wheelbarrow enables the worker to lift and transport much more weight than would be possible without the wheelbarrow. The long handle of the wheelbarrow acts as a lever. Attached to the wheel, the lever moves up and down. The fixed point where the lever meets the wheel is called the fulcrum. The barrow that holds the load sits atop the wheel. On one end of the load, a person exerts pressure (lifts) to move the lever (long handles). At the other end, the load in the wheelbarrow is lifted also. The distance between the wheel and the ends of the handles is greater than the distance

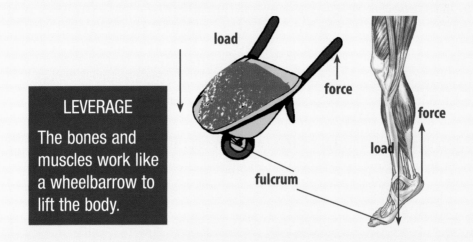

LEVERAGE

The bones and muscles work like a wheelbarrow to lift the body.

load

force

force

load

fulcrum

between the wheel and the load. That means the force needed to lift the wheelbarrow is much less than the force needed to move the load.

The bones and joints of the foot and leg operate in much the same way as a wheelbarrow. The bone serves as the lever, while the joint is the fulcrum. A girl standing on her tiptoes uses the lever system to lift the weight of her body. The joints in the toes serve as the fulcrum around which the bones of her feet (the levers) move. This provides the force to raise the body upward.

Wear and Tear

Like a house, the human body needs constant maintenance and repair. Bones, like other parts of the body, get rid of old, damaged cells and replace them with new cells. Special cells called **osteoclasts** continually break down bone fiber and dissolve it. These cells emerge from the bone marrow and apply acid to the bone. This makes a hole in the bone and releases some of the calcium stored there. Once that job has been done, other special cells called **osteoblasts** fill the holes with new tissue. The fibers absorb calcium, which hardens the new bone. **Hormones** and other substances in the body supervise the bone's remodeling project, telling the body where repairs are needed and how many new cells to produce. Hormones are chemicals released by glands and carried by the blood. They control the actions of certain parts of the body. A person replaces 10 to 30 percent of the skeleton each year.

Children's bones remain flexible while they grow. Because they are flexible, children's bones may bend rather than break during a fall. When the bone does break, it usually heals quickly.

As a person grows older, bones harden and become more brittle. Broken bones in a toddler may take six to eight weeks to heal. A person who is sixty or older may require several months for a broken bone to heal. Bones in some older people may never heal completely after a break.[1]

Older people, especially women, may have a disease called osteoporosis that causes the bones to break easily. Sometimes just rolling over in bed can cause a bone to break in a person with this disease. In these people, the osteoclasts break down more bone than the osteoblasts replace. People with osteoporosis constantly lose bone and calcium, and their bones become brittle.

Teenage girls who are too thin or have eating disorders may also lose bone minerals. This can increase their risk of broken bones and other health problems.

Several other diseases can affect the bones. Paget's disease causes bones to become enlarged and misshapen. People who have Paget's disease often have bone pain and fractures. They may also develop arthritis, another disease that affects the joints. Wear and tear can damage the cartilage, as is the case in osteoarthritis. Rheumatoid arthritis, a different type of disease caused when the body's immune system attacks the synovial fluid, also damages the joints. In both cases, the cartilage eventually wears away and bone rubs on bone. This is painful and makes it difficult to use the joints affected.

Osteogenesis imperfecta (OI) is a genetic disorder. This means a defect, or change, in the genes is passed down from parent to child. People with OI have weak bones because their bodies cannot produce enough collagen or the collagen they do produce is of poor quality. Some people with OI have had hundreds of broken bones for no apparent reason.

Tumors—masses of tissue—sometimes form in bones. Both benign (those that are not cancerous) and cancerous tumors replace healthy bone tissue with their own mass of tissue. Benign tumors, which are not fatal, do not spread. There are several types of bone cancer. One type forms tumors in new tissue as the bone grows. Other types of bone cancer produce tumors in nerve tissue in the bone marrow or in cartilage. Cancers that begin in other areas of the body, such as the breast or lungs, can spread to the bones through the bloodstream or the lymphatic system.

Skin Damage and Repair

Like bones, the skin constantly repairs and replaces old, dead cells. The outer cells that make up the skin die and flake off or wash off. Living cells in the lower part of the epidermis divide and push other cells to the skin's surface. These new cells take the place of the dead cells shed by the skin until they, too, die and are replaced. Dust that collects in people's houses consists mainly of bits of discarded skin. By the time a person reaches the age of seventy, he or she will have cast off about forty pounds of dead skin.[2]

When a teenager's body begins to mature, the body produces an extra supply of hormones. Often these hormones cause the glands in the skin to produce too much oil. The skin's pores become clogged, which causes acne.

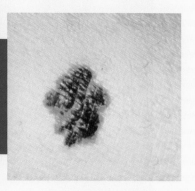

SKIN CANCER

Too much sun can cause skin cancer. At right, melanoma, the deadliest skin cancer, forms a lesion on skin.

As we have said, the skin provides a waterproof shield to protect the inner body. If the skin burns, the damaged shield can no longer keep moisture inside and germs outside. That is why burn victims often die from dehydration or infections. Even if only a portion of the skin is damaged—as little as 20 percent—the person could die from loss of water. If burns damage the deeper layers of the skin where new living cells are created, the body cannot replace the missing skin. Healthy skin from another part of the body or from a donor can be used to repair the damage caused by burns.

Many disorders and diseases affect the skin. Some problems cause only minor irritation of the skin, like poison ivy or mosquito bites. Other disorders have far more serious outcomes, like skin cancer or leprosy. Skin cancer develops when too much sunlight triggers changes in the skin's cells. These cancerous cells multiply rapidly and form tumors on the skin's surface.

The two most common types of skin cancer—basal cell carcinoma and squamous cell carcinoma—are usually easy to treat, if detected early, by removing the tumor before it spreads to other parts of the body. These tumors are produced by cells in the epidermis. Melanoma, the most deadly form of skin cancer, comes from pigment cells in the skin. It, too, forms tumors on the surface of the skin. This form of cancer is more likely to spread, but it can be treated successfully if removed early. People who have a lot of moles should look at their skin regularly and tell their doctor if they see any changes.

Muscle Disorders

A person is born with a fixed number of skeletal muscle cells. He or she will never grow more. But exercise can strengthen the muscles. Lifting weights or doing other exercises causes the muscles to develop more filaments and makes the muscles larger. This gives the muscle more strength and more force. Muscles that are not used for a period of time become thinner and lose their strength. If a person does not use a muscle for several months, some of the muscle fibers will die. The body cannot regrow the dead fibers. By exercising the muscle, however, the person can build up the remaining fibers so the muscle can be used again.

Defects in genes cause some muscle disorders. Muscle fibers are made up of several proteins, each with its own job to do. Some of these proteins have complex genes. If any part of the gene that governs one of these proteins has a flaw, a person may develop a muscle disorder. Muscular dystrophy results from defects in the gene for the protein dystrophin, which helps form the surface of the muscle. Without a good supply of dystrophin, the muscles weaken and waste away. People with muscular dystrophy gradually lose muscle tissue until, in some cases, they must use a wheelchair to get around.

Some disorders that affect muscles occur when the body's immune system makes a mistake and attacks the muscle or related body part. In myasthenia gravis, special cells designed to attack germs (antibodies) instead destroy receptors that collect a chemical needed to make the muscle contract. In inflammatory myopathies, another form of immune system disease, antibodies attack and destroy muscle fiber. Fibromyalgia, also an immune system disease, causes muscle pain and makes it difficult to sleep.

Amyotrophic lateral sclerosis (ALS), also called Lou Gehrig's disease after the ballplayer who had ALS, attacks the motor neurons. People with the disease have trouble moving because the neurons cannot transmit instructions to the muscles.

Metabolic diseases are caused by a genetic defect. Because of a flaw in a gene, the muscle cannot process energy from food. People with these diseases have weak muscles and tire easily.

Sports Injuries

Everyone needs to exercise for good health. But some people—especially young athletes—go overboard. Doctors report that more and more young people are injuring themselves while playing sports. Many of these young players spend three hours a day or more training or playing in games. They overuse muscles and put stress on growing bones. Athletes intent on playing don't give injuries time to heal.

Young athletes who overdo things are more likely to have stress fractures during a time when bones are still growing. The cartilage is also at risk. If too much stress is put on cartilage as it is growing, it can become damaged. Knees, ankles, and elbows are most apt to be injured by overuse.

Some sports injuries have become common enough to have their own name, such as Little League Elbow and Swimmer's Shoulder. In both cases, the person overuses arms and shoulders. If the problem is not treated,

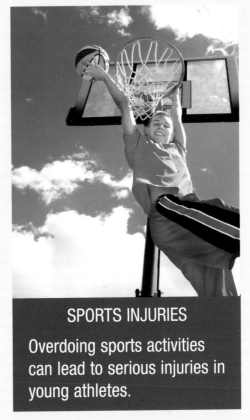

SPORTS INJURIES

Overdoing sports activities can lead to serious injuries in young athletes.

the person may need surgery. Other players break bones, pull muscles, tear ligaments, or damage joints.

More than 365,000 football and basketball players fourteen or younger received injuries that landed them in the hospital in 2009. Other high-risk sports included wrestling, boys' cross-country, girls' gymnastics, and soccer.[3]

As a result, sports injuries have become the leading cause of injury among adolescents. More than 3.5 million children 14 years and younger are treated for sports-related injuries each year.[4]

Staying Healthy

Chapter 5

As we have seen, the musculoskeletal system has an amazing array of features that protect it from harm. Waterproof skin wards off germs, bones protect vital organs, and cartilage cushions bone. Even so, the system occasionally breaks down or is overwhelmed by disease or injury. When that happens, the body may need help to repair the damage.

Staying in Shape

It is especially important to be active and eat foods with plenty of calcium when one is young. Healthy bones are developed in childhood and the teen years. By age twenty, people have accumulated most of the bone minerals needed for healthy bones.

After that age, people need to take steps to stop bone loss. Exercise is important for people of all ages. Lifting weights strengthens muscles and increases the density of the bones. Such exercise routines can increase bone density by as much as 8 percent a year.

Activities such as running, skipping, and jumping rope also increase bone density. Exercise and a healthy diet can prevent people from gaining too much weight. Extra weight puts stress on weak joints and muscles. Gentle exercise such as yoga or tai chi can help improve strength, balance, and

EXERCISE

Exercise and an active lifestyle help keep the body, bones, and muscles in good shape.

flexibility. These gentle activities are particularly important for people with osteoporosis, who can easily break bones if they fall.

Safe Sports

Young people who are active in sports need to take special precautions to prevent injuries. They should wear suitable footwear and use equipment that is in good condition. Wearing protective gear helps to prevent breaks and tears. It also makes injuries that do occur less severe. If injuries do occur, athletes should not play until the injury has healed properly. Playing while injured can result in an injury even worse than the original one.[1]

Young athletes also need to pace themselves and take breaks during practice and play. Doctors advise young athletes to get in shape gradually and allow plenty of time for rest. The "10 percent rule" provides a useful guide for sports fans: Training should not increase in length or difficulty more than 10 percent each time. Gentle stretching exercises should be done before beginning brisker activities. Doctors also urge young athletes to do several types of activities instead of focusing on one sport.[2]

KEEPING SPORTS SAFE
Proper equipment can help prevent sports injuries.

Healthy Inside and Out

Eating foods rich in calcium and getting plenty of sunshine are good ways to prevent bone loss. Milk, cheese, broccoli, almonds, dark leafy greens, and salmon all are good sources of calcium. Some people, especially older women, may need to take pills with calcium and vitamin D. Women past the age of fifty may take hormones to help keep their bones strong. Researchers are studying the effects of soy, which may also increase bone density.

While the sun provides needed vitamin D, its rays can also damage the skin. People can protect against cancer-causing ultraviolet rays by using sunblock of at least SPF15, wearing protective clothes and sunglasses, avoiding sunburns, and staying out of the sun at midday when the rays are strongest. Ultraviolet rays emitted by tanning booths and sun lamps can also damage the skin.

No Smoking, Please

Smoking is another thing to avoid. People who smoke are more likely to develop osteoporosis and have thin bones. Studies have also shown that the hair of smokers may turn gray earlier than the hair of people who do not smoke.[3] Both sunlight and smoking can age the skin, causing premature wrinkles. A new study found that smoking triggers a gene that destroys collagen, the protein that keeps skin soft and smooth.[4] It also interferes with blood flow to the skin.

Families with a history of diseases caused by genetic defects such as muscular dystrophy may be advised not to have children. Some medications may be able to combat the effects of a misguided immune system that causes certain disorders.

People with arthritis and other joint diseases may benefit from artificial joints. When a joint has been destroyed, surgeons can implant a new joint made of titanium or other strong metal. Scientists are experimenting with cartilage implants and hope someday to regrow damaged tissue in injured or diseased joints.

Awesome Anatomy

People may marvel at the intricate architecture that allows the Bayonne Bridge to support rush-hour traffic speeding across its 1,652-foot span between New Jersey and New York. But they have only to look down to see another wondrous arch that enables their feet to support their body's weight.

The sweeping towers of Westminster Abbey in London may take the breath away. But the structure of our own bodies is itself awe-inspiring. The flexible vertebrae keep us upright. Our muscles and bones allow us to move, run, skip, and smile.

Inventors have created huge mechanical claws to help lift heavy objects. But at the end of our arm, the hand can play the violin and retrieve a contact lens as well as lift barbells.

Builders may construct monumental structures out of concrete. But one cubic inch of healthy human bone can support the pressure of ten compact cars.

The body's musculoskeletal system works constantly at millions of tasks, keeping us moving, protecting us from harmful substances, supporting our weight. It also works with other body systems to keep us alive and healthy. The ribs protect the lungs and the respiratory system that do our breathing for us. The skin covers all the other organs of the body in a protective sheath. The muscles move our mouths so that we can eat.

The musculoskeletal system contains wonders that the world's scientists have yet to understand. But one thing they do know is that the body's structural system is truly one of the world's great wonders.

Amazing but True

Chapter 6

The most powerful muscles of the body are found in the legs.

A baby's skeleton has about 350 bones. By the time he or she becomes an adult, the skeleton contains only 206 bones because many of the bones fuse together.

At birth, the bones in a baby's skull are held together by flexible membranes. This allows the baby's head to compress and pass through the birth canal. By the time the baby reaches age two, the bony plates in the head fuse, forming a hard covering where the "soft spot" once was.

The hardest bone in the body is the jawbone.

The skin is the largest organ in the body.

An average person has more than five million hairs growing on his or her body at one time.[1]

The longest muscle in the body is the sartorius muscle. A flat, narrow muscle, the sartorius runs from the hip to the inside of the tibia (shinbone). The muscle got its name from the Latin word meaning tailor because the muscle allows a person to sit with legs crossed in a position used by tailors at work.

The body's smallest muscle—the stapedius—contracts to protect the inner ear. It takes about 40 to 80 milliseconds for the muscle to contract in response to a loud sound.

SMILE: Give your muscles a break.

The human body has more than six hundred muscles. It takes seventeen muscles to smile but forty-three muscles to frown.

The hyoid bone—a U-shaped bone at the base of the tongue—is the only bone in the body that does not touch another bone. Its job is to provide an anchor for the tongue's muscles.

The skeleton makes enough bone tissue every seven years to create an entirely new skeleton.

The spinal cord—which is about eighteen inches (45 cm) long and approximately three-quarters of an inch across (2 cm)—contains more than ten billion nerve cells.

BONE

One-third of bone is made up of water.

The human body has more skeletal muscle than any other tissue. Skeletal muscle accounts for about 23 percent of a woman's weight and 40 percent of a man's weight.

FUNNY BONE

The long bone that runs from the shoulder to the elbow is called the humerus bone, thus the term "funny bone." When a person hits the nerve next to the bone, he or she feels a tingling sensation. The bone's name comes from the Latin word *humerus*, meaning upper arm or shoulder.

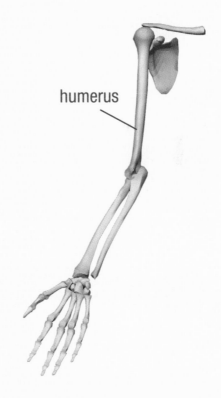

humerus

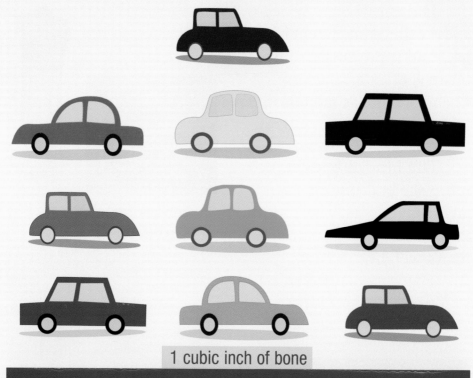

1 cubic inch of bone

SUPER BONE

One cubic inch of bone can support the weight of ten compact cars (18,000 to 24,000 pounds). Bones are four times as strong as concrete.

The spinal cord is less than two feet long and is as wide as a person's index finger. In that small space there are more than 10 billion nerve cells.

A person sheds more than half a pound of dead skin each year. By the time a person is seventy, he or she has shed forty pounds of skin.

The skin contains 2 to 3 million sweat glands, which produce 5 to 6 pounds of sweat an hour.[2]

Two million red blood cells die each second and are replaced by new cells produced in the bone marrow.[3]

Chapter Notes

Chapter One: What Is the Musculoskeletal System?

1. Alma Guinness, ed., *ABC's of the Human Body* (New York: The Reader's Digest Association, Inc., 1987), p. 160.
2. George D. Zuidema, ed., *The Johns Hopkins Atlas of Human Functional Anatomy*, fourth edition (Baltimore, Md.: Johns Hopkins University Press, 1997), p. 10.
3. *Innerbody*, HowToMedia, Inc., 1999–2011, <http://www.innerbody.com/htm/body.html> (January 24, 2012).
4. Guinness, p. 133.

Chapter Two: Who Is on the Team?

1. George D. Zuidema, ed., *The Johns Hopkins Atlas of Human Functional Anatomy*, fourth edition (Baltimore, Md.: Johns Hopkins University Press, 1997), p. 11.

Chapter Four: Wear and Tear

1. Alma Guinness, ed., *ABC's of the Human Body* (New York: The Reader's Digest Association, Inc., 1987), p. 184.
2. *Innerbody*, HowToMedia, Inc., 1999–2011, <http://www.innerbody.com/htm/body.html> (January 24, 2012).
3. "Sport and Recreation Safety Fact Sheet," Safe Kids USA, n.d., <http://www.safekids.org/our-work/research/fact-sheets/sport-and-recreation-safety-fact-sheet.html> (January 24, 2012).
4. Ibid.

Chapter Five: Staying Healthy

1. Larry Tye, "Injured at an early age: Competitive play, concentration on single sport, pushing of limits take toll," *Boston Globe*, Sept. 30, 1997, p. A-1.

2. John P. DiFiori, M.D., "Overuse Injuries in Children and Adolescents," *The Physician and Sportsmedicine*, vol. 27, no. 1, January 1999.

3. *What Is Osteoporosis?*, MSN Health, Microsoft Corp., 2001, <http://content.health.msn.com/content/dmk/dmk_article_40065MSN> (Sept. 6, 2001).

4. Christine Lahmann, Jörg Bergemann, Graham Harrison, Antony R. Young, "Matrix Metalloproteinase-1 and Skin Ageing in Smokers," *The Lancet*, vol. 357, no. 9260, March 24, 2001, p. 935.

Chapter Six: Amazing but True

1. *Innerbody*, HowToMedia, Inc., 1999–2011, <http://www.innerbody.com/htm/body.html> (January 24, 2012).

2. George D. Zuidema, ed., *The Johns Hopkins Atlas of Human Functional Anatomy*, fourth edition (Baltimore, Md.: Johns Hopkins University Press, 1997), p. 157.

3. Charles Clayman, ed., *The Human Body: An Illustrated Guide to Its Structure, Function, and Disorders* (New York: DK Publishing, Inc., 1995), p. 109.

Glossary

appendicular skeleton—The bones of the arms, legs, pelvis, shoulders, hands, and feet.

axial skeleton—The bones of the skeleton that run from the head and down the spine; includes the skull, the backbone, and the ribs.

axon—The stem-like part of a nerve cell that sends messages in the form of electrical impulses to the next cell.

ball-and-socket joints—Joints that allow the bones to move in a circle.

bursa—A small sac of fluid that lubricates the joint.

cartilage—Tough, smooth, elastic material in the joint that prevents bones from rubbing together.

collagen—Protein that makes up much of the connective tissues of bone, muscle, and skin and makes them flexible.

compact bone—Layer of hard, rigid bone beneath the periosteum.

dendrites—The part of a nerve cell that receives messages.

dermis—The inner layer of the skin.

epidermis—The outer layer of the skin.

extensor muscle—A muscle that contracts to straighten a part of the body at the joint.

flexor muscle—A muscle that contracts to bend a part of the body at the joint.

follicle—Sphere-shaped group of skin cells where hair forms.

gland—An organ that produces and releases a chemical that triggers a specific action in the body.

hinge joints—Joints that allow bones to move back and forth.

hormones—Chemicals released by glands and carried by the blood that give orders to certain body parts.

isometric contraction—Tensing of muscle during which the muscle does not shorten or lengthen.

isotonic contraction—Tensing of muscle that causes it to shorten or lengthen.

keratin—A tough protein that forms in dead skin cells and makes up the outer layer of skin.

ligaments—Tough, flexible bands of tissue connecting bones to other bones.

marrow—Fatty substance in the center of the bone that produces blood cells.

melanin—Dark granules that color the hair and the skin.

motor neurons—Nerve cells that carry messages to the muscles.

neurons—Nerve cells.

osteoblasts—Cells in the bones that replace bone.

osteoclasts—Cells in the bones that break down bone.

osteocytes—Bone cells.

periosteum—Thin outer layer of the bones.

sensory receptors—A nerve ending in the skin that receives information from the body and the outside world and transmits the messages to the brain.

skeletal muscles—Voluntary muscles attached to bones that allow the body to move.

smooth muscles—Muscles found in the body's internal organs; they are involuntary muscles.

subcutaneous layer—Layer of tissue that connects the skin to the muscle and bone.

synovial sac—Thin tissue that lines joints and contains fluid.

tendons—Thick cords of tissue connecting muscle to bone.

vertebrae—The thirty-three bones of the backbone.

Further Reading

Books

Haywood, Karen. *Skeletal System.* New York: Marshall Cavendish
Benchmark, 2009.

Johnson, Rebecca L. *The Muscular System.* Minneapolis: Lerner
Publications Co., 2005.

Rake, Jody Sullivan. *The Human Skeleton.* Mankato, Minn.: Capstone
Press, 2010.

Stewart, Melissa. *Moving and Grooving: The Secrets of Muscles and
Bones.* New York: Marshall Cavendish Benchmark, 2011.

Internet Addresses

Discovery Communications. Discovery Kids: Your Gross and Cool
Body - Skeletal System. 2000.
<http://yucky.discovery.com/flash/body/pg000124.html>

Nemours. KidsHealth.
<http://www.kidshealth.org>

Index